HIGH noon nepTune

David Groulx

BookLand
press

Published by
BookLand Press Inc.
15 Allstate Parkway, Suite 600
Markham, Ontario L3R 5B4
www.booklandpress.com

Printed in Canada

Library and Archives Canada Cataloguing in Publication

Title: High noon Neptune / David Groulx.
Names: Groulx, David, 1969- author.
Series: Modern Indigenous voices.
Description: Series statement: Modern Indigenous voices
Identifiers: Canadiana (print) 20240321316 | Canadiana (ebook) 20240321340 | ISBN 9781772312225 (softcover) | ISBN 9781772312232 (EPUB)
Subjects: LCGFT: Poetry.
Classification: LCC PS8563.R76 H54 2024 | DDC C811/.54 — dc23

Canada Council   Conseil des arts
for the Arts   du Canada

ONTARIO ARTS COUNCIL
CONSEIL DES ARTS DE L'ONTARIO
an Ontario government agency
un organisme du gouvernement de l'Ontario

Ontario

We acknowledge the support of the Government of Canada through the Canada Book Fund and the support of the Ontario Arts Council, an agency of the Government of Ontario. We also acknowledge the support of the Canada Council for the Arts.

HIGH noon neptune

Table of Contents

A poem agnosia

I have a poem stuck in my throat

I have a poem stuck in my fingers

I have a poem stuck in my liver

It waits for me to grow old and die,
to be released from me
and I, finally
from it.

Never knowing its notes, its nuances, or madness
but such is the nonsense of life,

dead stares.

A beauty never broken on my knuckles.
A word never smashed on my lips,
never knocked out, not even
technically.

Angel of the one last joy ride

You disappeared from me after that night
we stole a car
for the biggest song we ever stole
was four or five
cop cruisers we smashed into?
I do remember a short pistol
being pressed against the back of my head
"Get the fuck out of the car"
same said back sir!
and we were gone again
You disappeared from me that night
I remember being slapped around at the cop station
and then I lost you
or you lost me
I went down one road
looking for what I could find
You went down another
and I never saw you again
heard stories
about how you got into gangs
and into prison
and the last story I heard about you
being found in a hotel room
with a needle in your arm
going on one last joy ride
I guess some things fall faster than others
and sometimes the speed of light changes
and sometimes I find myself
back on these highways again
stopping at every light

signalling every lane change
growing old
driving
alone in the moonlight
and sometimes I think
if I could have ran backward
I would have kept on running

A night not at the hotel

I hope it is busy my love
but I am not there
to be there
ah to be there
when the boys gather
to drink pitchers of beer
and watch the football
talk of work
laugh
I will be here listening to a wasteland
what a waste
again, hoping
that the woman gather
to eat and talk
of men
the men talk too
of the work they have or didn't
I am not there
I will be here
listening to the mariner's
echo, held in his thin hand
that he gives to me
I hope you wear your hair
up
just like that
and all that change that jingles
in all those pockets and purses
go into your apron
that the doors swing open
always open and never close

I will not be sitting at the bar
I will not be sitting at the tables
I will be here, ebrious with brandy
and the waters of Alpheus
kiss me now, my dear
though I cannot see you
though I cannot touch you
kiss me now
and it will come to me
like a southern breeze
and warm what you cannot see
warm what you cannot touch
kiss me now

Looking at a shallow mistle thrush

I

Nothing is issued
and the ladies go blah
delicate and fierce
boom boom ah
a decision of
Gemini
a hand of illusion
can't be free
got a hard on for home
and I can hear myself speak
great Britannia
come up the stage
and glow
an old back of a
shallow fish
a skeleton maze
the evening gestured like this
a heap to shove off
there nothing but wine
the weather here is
getting a rain
and disappear from here
a kiss goodbye Gemini
must go like that
after awhile
see you waking after awhile
a decision of the dawn
to sop up what's left

of the darkness
but that's just here
looking at a choke
the stage that floats
and everything is old
my mania misplayed
again

II

Come and get this fire
I'll get you high
I'm just a little blue
a tired colour of my horn
the boots, the eye, and the avenue
sometimes, Lady I think of the night
making love, making ready
to leave
the phone rings, the smoke
the heel taps away and the moonlight
makes words
coming through
up to my shoulder
I froze
I was lame
another heart shines on
hurt
let me leave hungry
open another bottle of seems to be
and explanations
Miss Tabytha fly
you figure, you stumble

the horses will come
when you say please
please Miss Tabytha
every Sunday
apparently still
hand travelling
just to be alive

III

You wore my horn somewhere
I think I heard a train
in the mountains
there was laughter and a blade blond
and the love of footsteps
that we couldn't come up for air
I held it all in
like a man will always hold love
with both hands
My roads to you
became my favourite
but I gotta go around
just to get there
it was a scree
you and I
and the tombs we carried, swayed
I doubted the venom
but the venom did not doubt me
now I'm going there
my favourite roads but,
I gotta go around

IV

I was to become a withering
brought down to my muss
and I was almost
broken in two and nothing tasted good
does she ever low
something bubbles from her mouth
and I ain't sure why
anything just wearing on
and the goats are gone
I wait
and a crippled memory
comes back like a hand
feeling its way around in the dark
a blind
a kink
a trip down a crooked bone
I can hardly see
winding my way
just pigeon past
a sweet key
and it's been so long
since we crumbled
like frozen snow
in the rain
my your way to me again
I'm shining
following
especially you
like half hand of a steed
hurry to me

V

I got my body pressed against
another get away
got the wind in my hand again
leaving this dirty bastard town again
helplessly I'm pulled from
your blah blah blah
just get to the hoar-ra
in the front of you when you zoom bye
goin on the Z train
the starlight moves
all light moves
there is nothing that can turn me off
about anything I can get out of this
they line up everything
the sunshine keeps moving
the ooze are ahhhs
and a rustle at my feet

Maculate obscure

I suppose we are all damned to die
one way or another
but if I could choose
it wouldn't be on some foreign field
where the state could call me a hero
it wouldn't be on some dingy street in a fist fight
where they would say he died with his boots on
I wish it would be with you my love
holding me, my love
I wish it would be that way and not another
I wish it would be
with some witty thing said
and we both smile and
one of us cry because
one of us is leaving
my promise would be broken
but only because of death
it's a good excuse I suppose

I wish it would be this way and not another

Domestic harmony

If you don't come home
I wouldn't hold it against you
I wouldn't want to be with me either
ask my liver
seeing me drunk again
I cleaned the house
supper's made and the bills paid
I walked the dog
all my chores are done
I deserve a drink I say and it tasted so good
and now here I am drunk again
but supper's made and the dog walked
and the sun is setting
I'll drink to that
and if you don't come home
I'll wake somewhere in the night

wondering what else I could have done

The angel of the haruspex

The haruspex stared into the roads
of my famine, said it would be new
she said you would speak, she
said there would be two she
said there would be autumn
and its runes would bring your mouth close
she said at last your face would not tell me anything
she said your mouth would be a complete road
curved to affliction and feral dances
that stagger on the wild edges of my heart
she said, the gypsy said I would be drunk, I would be
branches, I would be evenings in maschera and alchera,
I would be drinking Dolcetto
lines and snorting curves, she said, the haruspex said
I would be generous and you
would not, that our hearts would be beating
like tenor drums
and you would forget me and everything and that only
I would remember
she said that you would not be at home till nightfall,
she said, with the starlight dripping down on me
she said the kisses, the kisses sometimes end,
she said that you would pierce
this in me, it would be like sleep
and that only I would remember
our country, and I do and the haruspex said I would
know how like I don't know now

and that our star would fall out of the night sky, she
said it would be the song that band played
and the starlight would lie at your feet
struggling to get up again and that it would always be
like this and be like this never
again, she said we would watch ourselves
from the future or ignore them later
she said, the angel of the haruspex said
that we were written on the stars
and we were written on the cards
down all the broken shards and the broken
she said we should whistle on with it and low heels
down all the broken avenues
and she said, said that you would always belong to me
and that I would
always remember it like the bruised veins
beneath my skin

Police station in a small town out west

A woman cop is taking my prints
and she makes me an offer after seeing
my wedding ring
"Take off your ring and I'll take you in the back cell
and show you what a real woman is."
She smiles at me and I remain silent
These people really are pigs

Different jail, different guard, different town

I am called from the range to the only door out
to have my picture taken, see I am a new inmate
and the screws need this in case
I am murdered or escape
away from the eyes of the other prisoners
I joke with the guards
I do this because I never take anything seriously
all the photographs of all the other prisoners
on the walls
look miserable, I suppose cause this is a miserable place
I asked the guard if I can smile when he takes my picture
I do and he does

we break a rule and we laugh together

[Deleted]

I cannot write this poem about you
to say,
I knew a young boy
a beautiful boy
a brown boy
a black haired boy
a brown eyed boy
who'd found his sister hanging by a rope in his closet
you see I cannot be unmuzzled
to un-gate my gate and
sometimes the truth cannot dangle from a tongue
cannot tell you of my failure
that short misery that faltered and shook
what I thought was unshakeable
I knew a young, wonderful boy
who carried a sadness that was heavier than the world
to say I was helpless
and saw it crush you
and I crumbled [deleted]
and watched it
tear down a young boy I knew
a wonderful boy
a brown boy
a black haired boy
a brown eyed boy
who was just a child

Dirt road broken

I grew up on a dirt road
where the corpses of spring rain

turned the road into mud
a meagre emptiness

what I found there
and what I kept there

skin has fallen
tears that I can only think of now

Angel of scarred wrists
Angel of highway bones

most of my friends
gone now

the rest
on their way

this road breaks/broke my heart
so easily

Typhoon's trigger

I can tell you what a man looks like
going down, passing out from a punch
It looks like he's fighting against a wind
coming up from the ground
his legs wobble
like he's drunk
eyes barely open
his legs give out
he hits the kitchen floor
his mouth closed
My father standing over him

Angel of larghetto

Sometimes you sound like Glenn Close
and sometimes like Helen Mirren
to me
and I like to hear you read or sing or just speak
that thrilling sin we commit
only with sound
that *ahhhhh*
that mmmmm
deep breathe my dear
deep breathe
into my ear
me a beast, a barbarian
my crashing heart
soothed by your voice
a garden surrounded by teeth and smoke
and one snake that taste like ashes
waiting for this small bird
Speak, and let me slide into your jaws
and die there

Scenes as a boy

I was out picking raspberries
for my mother to make raspberry jam
when I found a pot plant
I wanted to take home to my mom
I sold it to a guy standing nearby for a quarter
with my first drug deal
I bought candies
it was all profit

I stole a six pack of *Lonesome Charlie*
from the kitchen table
to the bush, drank it
alone
passed out
it said
Looking for a Friend?
on the box
and I guess I was

I found some hash on the dresser
it the room I shared with my older brother
I took it
rolled it up and smoke it
and then I laughed
watching him looking around the house for hours
he's going to kill me when he reads this

For the angel of the far off days

I

My mother slashed my father one night
with a knife she had bought him for his birthday
he took the knife away from her
grabbed a tea towel
wrapped his arm
and told her to sit down before she hurt herself
he leaned against the kitchen counter
finished his beer
and loved her like no other man could

II

My father knocked another man out
one punch
My father never said a word
he was a man of few
Why raise your voice when you could raise your
hand?

III

I came home one morning in handcuffs
My father answered the door
looked at me and said
get up stairs
One of the cops took the hand cuffs off
my dad began to close the door

The cop said
Don't you want to know what he did?
my dad replied
If it was that bad you wouldn't be bringing him home
and closed the door.

IV

He came home
from the mine one day with a broken hand
I asked him if it hurt
he said no
but that there was a young child crying in the
hospital while was there
and he asked god to take the child's pain
and put in his hand

V

I remember these things
but I remember this the most
coming home drunk climbing into his bed
and telling him I loved him
he put his arm around me
and I began to cry

VI

When he died
I wasn't there
at his final moments
I didn't want to be
I didn't want to see
the strongest man I knew
the man I had loved my entire life
wither and die
and I felt ashamed of myself

VII

I dreamed of my dad
not long after
He had come down from a ladder
and I asked him if he was ok
he said he was fine
and lifted heavy hells from my
hands

VIII

I was a child again
and my father was going off to work
in the mine
the house was quiet
and he gave me some cheese to feed a small
mouse that lived in our kitchen floor

Miss Paula's mom

How many times can my
heart break like this?
When does heartache become lethal
to put another cat down
to be sitting here waiting
and waiting, again and again
for you to die; it's too late now
for fishing or TV bingo
or any of that shit, it's almost
time to say goodbye

I'm tired and I'm stoned and
ah there, broken again
and I'm crying, dammit why
does this keep happening? Why
does this keep ~~fucking~~ happening
My dog who went to live on a farm
and never came back.
                    Did
he forget me? did he forget me?

My cat, who got caught the wrong way under a wheel
He might have said it.
                    And it breaks
again and again and again and again,
it's like a goddamn Ford
it just keeps breaking
then the tears start, I'm spewing
like a ~~fucking~~ fire hydrant.

It's
like I've never done this before.
My heart breaks, tears, you die more
tears, My heart breaks. You'd think
it would be routine by now
I'd get used to it. I never do
I am a virgin at death
like you
and you my father and you my mother
and you my friend
and for you Betty Boop.
For how many time my heart has broken and whatever
pieces are left to love you with
those are the pieces of my heart
I cherish the most

The angel that slept on steel

Yes dreams are good to have until the world takes
them and crushes
them into so many little shards
you cant' even use them to slit you
own wrists.

and yet you hang on to them
those little shards
like someone who hangs on to tuberculosis

what the hell's wrong with you?

I took all the furniture you left behind
burned it
drank beer
and got drunk on the ashes

My land lord is an eristic arse, not deserving of the hole
he says he'll do something and doesn't

My boss doesn't even know I'm alive
which is good cause I wish he were dead
There was a rat in the cupboard
I spayed him with sunlight
now he smells nice

The guy downstairs is slapping
his girlfriend around again
I hear her screaming
Somebody help me! Somebody please help me!
So I go through their door and he stops
She goes back a few days later

The other nieghbour is having a Christian prayer party
in his apartment
I drink beer alone, the singing
ain't bad

When tragedy becomes popular, everyone wants
to be a part of it in
some sad way.

There is a guy on the transit
he's gotta be over 300 lbs
his scooter straining under his weight
his belly hair sticking out from beneath his shirt
which reads Goodlife Fitness
I'm baffled
Instead of equality we settled for sameness.

Didn't win battle of the bards
and came home to
stomach flu
Now I got poetry coming out of both ends
Flush flush...flush-
flush...

I kept waiting for the road to move but it was me.

Lets finish the last of the Pernod
drink these memories and pass out
next to the walls we have built

The day I met you
the sun shone a little brighter
the moon hung a little closer to the earth
then it does now
flowers smelled sweeter
sky was more blue
grass greener
the nights not so dark at all
and the mornings too early

There are two hounds
one who's belly is always full
and the other

The guy upstairs is a miserable pick
he chews his rage like a cow its cud
and if he dropped
dead I don't think anyone would care

I hate Monday mornings
because Monday mornings mean failure

There is a hooker on my street and she asks
if I want a blow job
before work

She promises to be clean, quick and discreet and to
finish the old fashioned way. I love old fashioned girls

I'm walking down Montreal road to have a beer and
there's a guy punching himself in the face. Man he's
really giving himself a beating. *I wouldn't want to be him.*
I live for the moment and its just that moment
I feel alive and
I'm only 30 seconds away from it.
The rat is still here and I have begun to call him
ghost rat, a legend of Vanier.

I just want to put a little knife it
baby
just a little more

My poetry is as accessible to you as my land was
to your grandparents.

The best thing about my home town was the road
out of it
my best memory of my home town was leaving it.

Now we've razed the sadness from our coupes but
cannot remove it from memory.
wear them down till they become bone.

Law of motion.
who are rich tend to stay rich, those that are poor tend
to stay poor.

We no longer take promises
You and I we've grown old
too old for that
We let promises blow away like autumn leaves
like trash in the street
It is hope in a new breathe
and our last breathe
that we still believe

I will hold you till the darkness has ended
though winter grows old in your bones
until my life feels like the sun bursting

You can talk to anyone as long as you understand that
most people like to listen to themselves.

Every man thinks he is invincible
every man is certain his beliefs are correct
this is the cause of conflict

The only difference between you and me is the amount
of gold on the casket.

Here there are no answers, but the is meaning.

If you want to know what a barroom taste like
kiss me.
The woman in this neighbourhood are mostly
white and fat
and all the children are
half black
this is what poverty looks like
domestic
half white

You wouldn't come down this way
you may drive by it on your way to someplace better
than this.

I am thinking the state wants me to feed it, with
whatever mash its turned my brain into.

I can only walk now with Lou Reed's songs and
my hands holding it's loneliness. that time can be
measured by shades of light and in this we give the
most attention to some other's holocausts, this way
we don't have to look at our own.

I think my poetry is killing me
You know I smoke a lot when I write
same when I drink
You once said I should quit smoking
that the world needed to hear me
Like I need to hear you now
There were so many things I wanted to say to you
Well, not really, I just wanted to say one thing
I guess there really is no point now,
is there?

My martyrdom is hidden in the mud, saved there
and walked through
I am bound to it
by it I am lashed to the land
a hook, barbed
It cannot be taken out of me

Capitalism has created a man who has become a
defect of nature, a parasite of the earth.
War has become a commodity.
In capitalism man has created his own predator.

Life is marked by a sequence of catastrophes
with order
the earth has its own order
its own history
a meaning
we cannot understand

One time stones and trees had power,
then someone made them into money
now their power has become twisted,
deformed.
For a man, his only
gift to his family
is his labour.

Poetry is the way I chose to help heal the universe
I am a scar on the place I live
I am a non-union poet.

What kind of person do you have to be
to fall in love? What if all you know is sacrifice,
can anyone fall in love
with someone like that?
When I was a child they said I enjoyed my own
company too much

Was it wrong?
Marching to the beat of my own drummer
my own creation
They said I hardly ever spoke as a child
so much noise already in my head
They put me in special education
failed me
Could you love someone like that
all those warmer summers
ago?
God was two lambs
there were two lambs
one was lost to the valley
one was lost to the city
one was lost to the fire
That was god.

Where the hands of time grasp our memories
and the dust slips through our fingers.
We have written our stories on the
rocks
That the rocks may know us
as their grandchildren.

My life rises in the east and falls

These years lay broken against the north of my soul.
I've had guns pointed at me twice in my life, both
times by the cops. The first time I felt the barrel
pushing against the back of my head, I still ran. The
second time pointed at my chest, funny thing is I was
not afraid, I just wanted to feel something.

My friend Matthew died in a hotel room in Barrie
from an overdose of cocaine
My friend Mark hung himself in his basement
in Edmonton
My friend Luke choked to death on his vomit
after a night of drinking
My friend John blew his brains out in his shed
My friend Peter froze to death after being
chased by the cops,
lots of questions there.
There were prayers I suppose
Food, cigarettes, and booze into the fire, but
mostly there have been deaths
and I've changed the names, there
have been deaths, but these were my friends
and none of them were older than I am now
when I take to the brandy and I take a slumber
I remember them.

Heaven was invented by a guy
who would never go there to
make poor people feel better about poverty.

God was created/invented by a man with a small penis.
Universities are the original bastions
of unoriginal thought.

The state only lives in our imagination, that's where real
power comes from,
The purity of virginity was again invented by a man
with a small penis.

Why do men wash there hands after pissing?
A cock is probably the cleanest part of his body,
the hands
probably the dirtiest. You should wash your hands
before you touch your cock
or just stop pissing on them.

People who ride bikes think that people who drive cars
are arseholes
People who drives cars think that people who rides bikes
are arseholes
They are all arseholes.

The difference between the rich and the poor is
that the poor know
it,
rich are oblivious.
but I have seen the living and the dead and to me,
there is no
difference.
Prayer was God's gift to the poor
Gold, his gift to the rich.

The house I spent my childhood in was torn down
like my childhood.

I tried to avoid it, turns out it was unavoidable.

writing poetry does not get easier as you get older, it
gets harder
time begins to disappear, you become humane
with words and
hate yourself for getting old

We are like German Shepherds
we are intelligent enough to obey orders
and the Master tells us
we are intelligent
and we think we are
obey orders

Canadians are fine with reconciliation
as long as they don't have to do anything
as long as it doesn't inconvenience them
as long as Indians stay out of their neighbourhoods

The sound of my voice is the sound of the earth
the colour of my skin is the colour of the land
I belong here.

I find myself drinking
beside the ditch
where you left our kisses
my mouth
a lonely distance to you

I am one of twenty
I know a history of you
where you call down this darkness
I remember the space
without you here
I know what you cannot believe
I am one of twenty
a sip a touch a flash

love is the only proof we have
that we are not alone.
They say if you drink alone
you're an alcoholic
so here's to you and to us
looking in the mirror

I dreamed someone was drinking my wine last night
St. Jude, the patron saint of lost causes.
and letters to Ziggy Stardust
that sleeping train
caught birds with one eye

"And the inhabitant shall not say, I am sick: the
people that dwell therein shall be forgiven their
iniquity." Isaiah 33-24

Sometimes when I'm half asleep I can smell bear
grease.
Combed short hair of the moon, the earth breathing
watch the castrated embers
seeping hard into the concrete
blood, piss and the echoes of a gun shot.

I am rising on low wings.
I was Apollo
who built this song
dreamed the world
and washed your body in the music
I commit this love
to the clouds in a glass of absinthe
where I keep the last kiss from my father
and my first broken heart
lumber through this pilgrimage
this fomenting ritual

Every time we made love I heard you say, "I felt some
of my life leave me, bring me to your darkness, where
there are two dogs".

The angel that woke

I

I am pushing into you and the water washing over
us like a new rain. And outside the door life goes on,
this place of dying, the living hate, especially me, this
place that struggles to make order of death.
I take the things I've brought from home
the shampoo, conditioner, soap,
let the water fall over you
these small moments are Lucullan for us
a sadness that becomes wet
"The door is locked, baby"
your mouth whispers that prayer
that was never wrote
"The world disappears when I'm with you, baby"
begin with my fingers touch with your lips
your tongue witching my body
there is only us
now
And we go from that moment
a flicker of hunger
stroked all the way to the lyric of lust
that shines on the verge
I comb your hair
long straight and curls over your breast
help you with your hospital gown
outside the nurses the patients
utter in broken voices like echoes
through a frost in a graveyard.

II

Now alone in this bed
I miss your kisses the most
lightly on my back
asking
You are confined to your chair
the prison your body has become
has ordered us to sleep alone
I miss you beside me
the punishment unbearable
the sentence unbreakable
the nights are vicious
feasts on us and masticates all of my sleep
I can hear it chewing us apart
and I miss you beside me
your kisses the most.

III

This is when we began dying and this is also
when you promised you wouldn't and
I believed you
and the light of your words wrapped around me
like a child rapt in wonder
I believed it
when you said you didn't want to free
I believed in your kisses and your urges
I believed in your prayers of evasion
and the master plan
I believed in your war and not your peace

My devotion to your coiled snake
I was faithful to your desolation
I embraced your invidious mordancy
for a life of Sundays I sat in my pew leaning on the
future that never happened
There are four canes/one for the angel of low taste/
one for the angel that staggers/one for
the angel of the raised eyebrow/one for the angel
of maigre days.

IV

Your fauvist heart, you brought to me
by a restless iron mantle
and your coronations became a coronach
and fantasies of war
mania and blessed our battles with our tongues
My heart was a rampage for you
like Hector charging into the Argives, We both
knew this rattle snake heart was meant for ruin
that shone in your words
that glistened in your whispers
that was lambent in your prayers
your bony kisses are milk and honey
that pale, miserable hound and ashen snow gathered
around us.

V

Your garrotting my Apician and boisterous heart,
like a deity
I make libations to in the dawn of days.
Who is the god of these devoted highways that
always lead me back to you?
Canonize me, bring me my grace, faithful to your
marcescence
I am sincere to you as a mouse to cat
I hold you in my mouth
our joy is deep and heavy.

VI

I watch as your body becomes your truculent prison
here my canorous and hollow vessels
breaking one by one
complete in our incompleteness
our lives flayed from their bones
parts of me become hard
take your hand from your mouth
quivering like a rabbit no one will hear you
divagate to the early flutter
I rove over your body
with my tongue
an echo of a swallow of every drop of you
the pleasure of long luciferous kisses
I am crashing to you
largo legato crescendo.

VII

My love is frost howling and my fields
are gaunt from a
winter that stumbled and begged to leave
what was born in spring was wiped away
the murky winter light against the snow
my words your words our words
stiff and cold on our tongues
a thin malice thawing.

VIII

Say yes to this night
yes to the music
yes to the brandy
say yes to the cigarette smoke
say yes to that ache
that time cannot consume
Say yes to this
blood this hair this body
yes to the deep blue,
sew this hollow abyss
we pull mandragora roots
and dance as one to the noise they make
we gather stones to rebuild the walls of a
strong city
we drink
we go by moonlight
our steps
coiled together
larghetto.

Aphelion and aphelions

I read what is broken
I recognize what is wounded
I've outlived most of my friends
witness to the number of lives we'd lived
I guess that's good enough
I've seen the useless grow old
and become more useless

Multiculturalism
is a fragmentation of society
to the benefit of the state
that it may eat

the Victorians
invent segregation

we are no longer defined by what we produce, but
what we consume

It was God who broke Lazarus
When he was a child
he wanted to become
an Indian leg farmer
and he could go as
Foucault to the wind
he didn't though
he just became an Indian leg farmer

As for Indians being nomadic
White people travelled here?

Poetry is raw meat
for the most primitive parts
of the soul
You've made me into cat
that kissed you while you slept
and
the highway is full of cats that couldn't count
and then I spoke to the saints
and then to the beasts
meow

I am late for the bus
to school
I stop running
I don't want to be stopped by the police
for running
This is the way it is for Indians
in Canada

Note on the fridge door

I keep my lung in the freezer
in a zip lock bag
Marked lung
I want it burned with me when I die
Please don't forget it

P.S Please take it out of the bag.

Aching through the darkness

I almost killed a man once
I wanted to touch him with a bullet
the rifle was loaded and everyone was drunk
but someone pulled the gun from of my hands
before I could change life
I followed the thunder in those days
chased it till I was empty
and now when I close my eyes
all I see are the flashes
of a distant lightning

I was recently asked to sit on a jury
to judge books
not written by
Indians
I was not asked to sit on
Gerald Stanley's or
Raymond Cormier's
jury
because they were accused of
killing Indians
Like the stars aching through the darkness
the settles are narrowed by the names given to the
living

Its twice this month I've taken a plane
from Ottawa to Toronto
and twice I've been pulled out of line
for a "random security check"
I'm beginning to think these things are not so "random"

I owned a 9 mm pistol once
and thought about killing someone
I traded it for two ounces of Lebanese red
because it was hotter than the steam pipes of hell
I got stoned on the hash and thought about
loving something else

I've built you a tempestuous edge
and songs about plutonium bombs
our living is only believing we exist
to guide each others shadows
through the flash

An angel of the twisting

I tried to hang myself once
it was new years eve in a hotel room
I tore the electrical cord from the TV and tied
around a shower nozzle in the tub
I didn't want to make a mess someone else
had to clean up
I let my naked body slide down the wall of the tub
feeling myself being suffocated ah no more pain no
more laughter no more anything
and then the ~~fucking~~ nozzle broke off
I wanted to die
Happy new year!

An angel wither and a narrow sonofabitch

I down my last two beers from my duffel bag
I'm leaving my home town again
I can't handle this relationship anymore
it cripples me
its too narrow
and I sever it with my thumb
and my fist
I hitch hike to the next city
and have a couple of beer at the bus depot
staving off a vicious hangover
I get back on the road and in the next city
I stop in at the Empire hotel
and have 3 scotch and a beer
and on the road again
a guy stops I get in
its a beater car, but the guy has a couple of mickeys
we drink we talk he lets me off in the next town
its dark now
everything is closed
all the booze is gone
and the hangover that's been stalking me
the one I've tried to stay ahead of is roaring down on me
A car stops, it a French couple
all I can understand is "Montreal"
oui I say
My hangover holds down me in the back seat
darkness

I'm sweating and freezing at the same time
I see wonted shadows of rats and spiders mostly and
others
I can't make out
all I can feel is I'm gonna die here
and no one will know where I'm going
or where I came from
or what was haunting me
or what I was running from
another dead Indian
died of the drink
rats and spiders crawling, rats and spiders crawling
and other things I can't make out.

Goodbye you narrow sonofabitch!

To the angel that slept under the loading dock

behind the beer store in an orange shag rug and shared
all of her beer with all the passersby who were on there
way to the fields that led to the old Canadian National
and the Nash before Afghanistan before Bosnia and
Libya and Iraq changed our world and everything we
though we knew about it.
There are people I wish would
descend
people I've thought about killing

too many people
too many times

The guy who cut me off
with the Baby on board sign
and that guy with the dream catcher
hanging off the rear view mirror
and that old lady counting out her nickels
at the cashier in front off me
a couple on nieghbours
and the guy whining about his parking space at Wal-Mart
and ...
you get it.

Angel of the black eschars

I met a beautiful woman
who had been raped
at I party I forgot to leave
Her abuser passed out in a room above
she came down the stairs
and began crying in my beer
Her tears were yellow
I could not take them out
so I drank them bitter and warm
Her face was painted in the mourning
of war and I smoked
cigarette after cigarette
and set her words in the smoke
for whatever song I could give her
and took her away from that place
it was all I could do.

The midnight grows merciful to us
and I drift in and out of moonlit comas

An angel of the monnet

This place is scheduled for
destruction soon
You see all places are
in this place
Well... you found it late in the light
but its not too late in enjoy its last luciferous shimmer
flaying that will soon
be extinct
No, no there will not be any pictures
they are not allowed at this stage and there
is no time for that anyway
You see I had waited for you, nursing my beer and
sipping my
drinks
I'm glad I did
cause now we can see the end
together
alone I must go
watch the tracers my dear
they're not pretty but they do
shine like neon across the world

Like Babylonian king lonely on his stump
in a cage made of red
I keep your memories from falling
into the waters of Lethe

The bees had thunder
in those days and the
birds had horns
the honey I made
was of flower's vibration on the tongue
& the beginning of a raindrop

Do not forget me
my love
I'll be here
drinking the last of the Monnet

A belief in a relationship with God
is a belief in violence
this is an illusion
that salvation comes
through domination
and not knowing
this is an illusion
like they have the faith
like they have a remedy for death

I was like a dog dancing
to a song the cats played
I love you
like a fog rising in
night

Angel of the grenades

I had a lover once
she slept in the backseat of my
car
while I drove around the city
looking for someone I could never find
she carried hand grenades in her pocket
Just in case she said
The truth is I wanted her the ~~fuck~~ out of my car
I couldn't follow her dreams
There was too much mileage on them anyways
but she had those ~~fucking~~ hand grenades
and she knew where all the bootleggers lived
and kept me from my illusions

We cannot live in our unconscious
We cannot live in our memories
We must always be grasping the mystery
that is life
that is everything

Two poems about becoming another being

Look at me!
I am becoming a bird
a winter bird
come
Not because we desire it but
because it is necessary
to become a bird

The land was easier to travel back
then
And there was no longer singing back
then
You see that was the time I wore deer
antlers
and now it sometimes feels to me
when my head is heavy
that I was in some other beings
dream
There arsehole nieghbour from upstairs
is chasing the gay guy downstairs because
the music is too loud
its probably not because the music's too loud
but that it's disco

Seeing the angel of beatings and the beaten

I saw this boy I used to go to school with
living on the streets of Toronto
while I was visiting there
I wanted to say hello give him a few dollars
but I didn't
I didn't want to embarrass him
I remembered that we learned
how to smoke dope together
remembered how he loved hockey
it was grade six I think
I remembered that he looked like his mother
a small beautiful red headed woman
I remembered that his stepfather would beat him for
the smallest wrong
I remembered the bruises
I remembered him telling me
that he'd run away one day
I guess he did
and all these years later
I watch him disappear into the street
carrying his stepfather in a knapsack

We should write beautiful things on paper
because trees always wanted to be beautiful
and the laws we write down should be good laws
in honour of them

Why do we call men who carry guns peacekeepers?

The angel of the fish in my belly

The angel that wanted to hold every sad thing
in the world in her arms
The angel that never wanted to stop rain and a song
from the Broken Bones couldn't save you
The angel who got drunk with the poets in the city
The angel of the fish in my belly
who left her prints and her shadows
on every wall in my house
the angel that took all the guns from my hands and
left the memory of the violence of it all to haunt me
The angel of every broken grace
the one that held me down in the spit
of the serpents mouth
till I could almost taste the eponyms of
the rivers
that was struck by the ptisan bands of lightening
The angel of the overdose and the fissure
leaving what is left behind buried
The angel who tied me up with her lips
who showed me what it was like to live
with only one horn.

Dear brother

Dear brother did you bring the baby
some peanut butter
his belly is aching and empty
and mother & father are gone

Dear brother the government's coming
coming to take us away
from each other and
I hate to see you beaten down with a paddle
for telling them to go ~~fuck~~ themselves
which is exactly what they should do

Dear brother I need to tell you, none of this is your fault
you are only five years older than me
I don't need to forgive you Dear Brother
but I need you to forgive yourself
and
I want to thank you
My brother who could swim like a fish
from your brother who could run like a deer
Chi megwetch

The many go before...

Angel of the soldier's eyeball
Angel of tenebrous candles
Angel of what the cat dragged in
and this restless thin
life has made me
Angel of the painted days
wonder back to me
meander this way again
grace this empty place again
stop me from feeling like midnight
all the time
Angel of being alone
Angel of all the broken stars
listen,
I knew two guys once, boys
who divided themselves from their memories
by falling beneath the wheels
of eighteen wheelers on highway 17
I went to their funerals
we were only boys
and we saw there
Angel of scarred wrists
Angel of playing in the rain
and my loneliness
Angel of phones that don't ring

Angel of birds that don't sing
tomorrow is always calling
an angel of broken hope
Angel of the sadness of the world
listen,

I had a friend once who froze to death
on a lake in Northern Ontario
the cops left him there for dead
and his brother found his bruised body
there three days later
We knew the cops were involved
but, nothing ever came of it
because the cops were white and we
we just Indians
Angel of injustice and the light that falls
of the skin that is fallen and the tears that I think
bring me the wind
and requite it
for this spoon of bitterness
for St. Anne, St. Remy
and all the dammed saints and
all children I knew
that are now dead.
Whisper into you folded hands to the
Angel of the rough-looking
been had
and hungry and
the seasons that fall on
a broken masterpiece

and the sins I've been faithful to
and the hour, that hour
when I should be forgiven and forgotten
My mind drifts away to days
that have fallen away from me

      The end is always deep
      and most men drown
      in six inches of water

Six inches of water

Till you ended up in places
you didn't want to be
with people you didn't want to be with
because they were like you
just holding your head above the water,
hang the mirror now my love,
I am ready to look at it
and it looks back at me,
echo apostasy
rattles the rein soughing
rouses me to wake

life was made uncommon drunks like us,
the days have blown away like leaves storms,
bring firelight
kiss me,
I swim the light around you
heaving on the notes
dragging whatever drink I have across the tables, while
the poets of Virgo outside, swaying to 97% of the
moonlight.

Also by David Groulx

- *Solus Urger Voyager*
- *The Windigo Chronicles*
- *Rising with a Distant Dawn*
- *Imagine Mercy*
- *From Turtle Island to Gaza*
- *Under God's Pale Bones*
- *Wabigoon River Poems*
- *These Threads Become a Thinner Light*
- *In the Silhouette of Your Silences*
- *When Angels Slept on Steel*
- *The Long Dance*